D0412660

n indfulness
on the go

mindfulness
on the go

DISCOVER HOW TO BE MINDFUL WHEREVER
YOU ARE—AT HOME OR WORK, ON YOUR DAILY
COMMUTE, OR WHENEVER YOU'RE ON THE MOVE

ANNA BLACK

CICO BOOKS
LONDON NEW YORK

For all those who show up and practice. Remember,
"you don't have to enjoy it—just do it!"

This edition published in 2019 by CICO Books
an imprint of Ryland Peters & Small Ltd
20–21 Jockey's Fields, London WC1R 4BW
341 E 116th St, New York, NY 10029

www.rylandpeters.com

First published in 2017 as a book and card boxed set

10 9 8 7 6 5 4 3 2 1

Text © Anna Black 2017, 2019
Design and illustration © CICO Books 2017, 2019

The author's moral rights have been asserted. All rights reserved. No part
of this publication may be reproduced, stored in a retrieval system, or
transmitted in any form or by any means, electronic, mechanical,
photocopying, or otherwise, without the prior permission of the publisher.

A CIP catalog record for this book is available from the Library of
Congress and the British Library.

ISBN: 978-1-78249-722-6

Printed in China

Editor: Helen Ridge
Design concept: Emily Breen
Illustrator: Amy Louise Evans

Commissioning editor: Kristine Pidkameny
Senior editor: Carmel Edmonds
Art director: Sally Powell
Production controller: David Hearn
Publishing manager: Penny Craig
Publisher: Cindy Richards

CONTENTS

INTRODUCTION 6

chapter 1:
about mindfulness 8

WHAT IS MINDFULNESS? 10

HOW MINDFULNESS CAN HELP 13

TEASING APART OUR EXPERIENCE 22

THE LIGHT OF AWARENESS 23

THE POWER OF THE BREATH 24

BREATHING INTO 26

TUNING INTO 27

TURNING TOWARD ALL EXPERIENCE 28

BEING WITH 30

THE POWER OF THE BODY 32

NOTICING THE NARRATIVE 34

CORE ATTITUDES 36

ABOUT PRACTICE 44

CORE PRACTICES 52

chapter 2:
activities and practices 62

ABOUT THE ACTIVITIES AND PRACTICES 64

THE ACTIVITIES 68

THE PRACTICES 95

REFLECT ON YOUR EXPERIENCE 122

FIND OUT MORE 124

INDEX 126

ACKNOWLEDGMENTS 128

INTRODUCTION

The phrase "mindfulness on the go" might seem
a contradiction. However, we can cultivate mindfulness
in more ways than just sitting still, and this book will
show you how.

People who already practice mindfulness often find it challenging to take the skills learned while meditating "on the mat" into their everyday life—the busy-ness of the office or family is distracting and they fall into familiar patterns of automatic behavior.

We can find ourselves compartmentalizing mindfulness into something we do at home for 15 or 20 minutes at a time, rather than face the challenge of doing it throughout the day. This book has been designed to encourage you to practice mindfulness anywhere and at any time. The more you do it, the more it will become second nature, and you will find yourself practicing it instinctively throughout your day.

Whether you have never meditated before or do so regularly, I recommend you read Chapter 1 first because it explains what mindfulness is and its origins, and how it can help us in our everyday lives. The focus is primarily on how to practice mindfulness, both formally and informally. It helps to be familiar with the terms used.

o **Teasing Apart Our Experience** (see page 22) explains what makes up our experience.
o **The Light of Awareness** (see page 23) explains how we can use our attention to explore our experience.
o **The Power of the Breath** (see page 24), **Breathing Into** (see page 26), **Tuning Into** (see page 27), **Being With** (see page 30), and **The Power of the Body** (see page 32) explain how we can use the breath and body as vehicles for our attention, helping us to access and relate to our experience in a different way.

o **Turning Toward All Experience** (see page 28) explains how mindfulness teaches us to be with all our experiences (even the ones we would rather not be with).

o Much of our suffering is self-created. We weave complex stories about our experiences, which we continually replay and embroider in our minds, thereby influencing our mood and behavior. **Noticing the Narrative** (see page 34) explains how we can free ourselves from believing these stories and thereby free ourselves from unnecessary suffering.

There is also information on the key attitudes to cultivate (see pages 36–43), guidance around practicing (how to take care of yourself, paying attention to your posture and managing discomfort, and dealing with the wandering mind—see pages 44–51), and core meditation practices (see pages 52–61).

Chapter 2 offers a variety of exercises, divided into activities and practices, that are all designed for you to be able to use daily and "on the go." You can find out more about them on pages 64–67.

chapter 1

about mindfulness

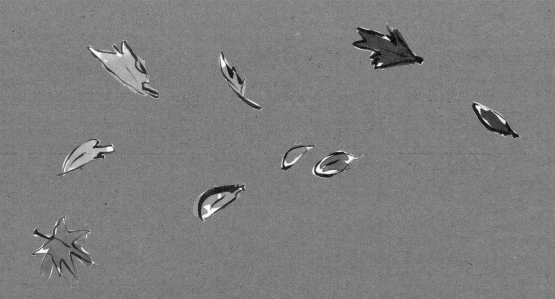

WHAT IS MINDFULNESS?

Mindfulness is commonly defined as deliberately paying attention to your experience as it unfolds, without judging it. Bringing kindly awareness is crucial.

When we practice mindfulness, we use our attention like a flashlight, shining it onto our experience (see The Light of Awareness, page 23).

Our **experience** refers to changing internal states, such as thoughts, physical sensations, and emotions (see Teasing Apart Our Experience, page 22) and includes how we relate to them as well as to our external experience, such as sounds, smells, other people, and our immediate environment. These internal and external factors are all interconnected.

We are interested in how we relate to our experience: wanting more of it, resisting it and trying to make it go away, or tuning out from it. Much of our suffering arises as a result of not liking what is arising and trying to make it different.

How we pay attention is important. Intention is crucial—we deliberately choose to pay attention to our experience and, most importantly, we pay attention without judging and with a dollop of kindness, if possible. These are two of the core attitudes we deliberately cultivate through practice and which are also cultivated by practicing regularly (see pages 37–39).

One of the ways mindfulness helps us is by teaching us to be with whatever arises. We don't chase a particular experience. We don't pick and choose and only pay attention to those parts we like (see Turning Toward All Experience, page 28). Paradoxically, it is only when we accept things as they are—that is, we stop resisting our experience—that our relationship to that experience changes. We learn to do this by accessing The Power of the Breath (see page 24) and The Power of the Body (see page 32) and by cultivating specific attitudes (see pages 36–43). Other benefits are described on pages 13–21.

Mindfulness is a natural trait that we all have to some degree. Children are inherently mindful but it is a trait that we often lose as we grow older. We can cultivate mindfulness through meditating, either formally or informally.

Formal meditation refers to meditation practices such as sitting, movement (for example, yoga or walking), and body scans. There are different variations and types of practice within each of these. Formal practices are commonly done at a chosen place, at a particular time, and for a certain duration. There are instructions for some formal practices on pages 52–61.

Informal meditation refers to practices integrated into our everyday life. This means doing an activity and knowing what we are doing while we are doing it, rather than thinking about something else or multitasking. For example, eating a meal mindfully can become a meditation. The majority of practices in Chapter 2 are informal practices. Some of them are mini meditations and others are more about developing an awareness of habitual patterns of behavior.

It is recommended that you explore a combination of both formal and informal practices. The former can be kept quite short if time is pressing. Both types of practice are beneficial and cultivate different things as well as supporting each other.

It is important that you explore your experience for yourself, rather than take anyone else's word for it—and do take care of yourself (see page 45).

ORIGINS OF MINDFULNESS

Mindfulness has its roots in Buddhism and has been practiced for over 2,500 years. However, its secular form was developed by Dr. Jon Kabat-Zinn and his colleagues at the Center for Mindfulness at the University of Massachusetts Medical School Hospital, USA.

Kabat-Zinn wanted to find a way to help people learn to live with chronic health conditions and the associated psychological problems, such as depression and anxiety. In the late 1970s he developed an eight-week program called Mindfulness-Based Stress Reduction (MBSR).

Since then, this program has been adapted to help people with a range of specific medical and psychological conditions, including cancer, anxiety, depression, eating disorders, and addiction. These adapted forms of MBSR—each with a specific name, such as Mindfulness-Based Cognitive Therapy (MBCT) for the prevent of relapse in depression—are commonly taught in groups where the specific vulnerabilities of the group will be addressed and the teacher will have experience of that particular context. This is unlike a general MBSR group, where people may be attending for lots of different reasons. In both contexts the focus is on how we relate to our problems rather than the problems themselves.

As the benefits of mindfulness were revealed (see opposite), people became interested in how to use it in a nontherapeutic context. Today, mindfulness is practiced in many areas of society, including schools, prisons, the sporting world, and the workplace.

Although mindfulness is commonly taught in groups (and that can be a really helpful way to establish your own personal practice), it is perfectly possible to practice on your own, particularly in the informal manner emphasized here. If you are practicing on your own without the support of a teacher, do pay particular attention to the cautions on page 45.

HOW MINDFULNESS CAN HELP

People come to mindfulness for many different reasons. Sometimes they are looking for ways to manage a chronic health condition, such as pain, depression, or anxiety, or they may want to learn to meditate or simply be more present in their life.

Certainly the evidence suggests that we are all more distracted, with many of us leading complicated lives, perhaps juggling family demands with work, which can be physically and emotionally draining. Whatever the reasons, it seems that people get out of mindfulness what they most need, as it helps each of us to find a better balance in our lives.

Mindfulness is not a magic cure-all that will make all our problems go away. However, it can help us to relate to our problems differently. Studies have shown that as well as psychological changes, physiological changes take place as a result of practicing mindfulness meditation, and these include changes in the brain as well as blood pressure and an improved immune system.

Reducing stress

It is common for people to report feeling less stressed after mindfulness meditation. The level of stress we feel is determined by whether we believe our resources are sufficient for the demands placed on them. Therefore, if we can change our perception of whether we are able to cope, we will feel less stressed. This is supported by the neuroscience that shows that the amygdala (the area of the brain that activates the stress reaction) is less active in those practicing mindfulness. Mindfulness also activates the body's internal calming response, which is the antidote to the stress reaction activated whenever we feel threatened.

Letting go of additional suffering

How we perceive our experience is determined by our interpretation of
it—the story we create about it. This story is often the source of much of
our suffering (see Noticing the Narrative, page 34). While we often can't do
anything about the original issue, we can do something about the extra stuff
we pile on top. Once we realize that a lot of our suffering is self-created, the
skills we learn through practicing mindfulness help us to let the stories go.
They may still come into our minds but we do not believe that they are true.

For example, if we can't sleep, we might lie awake worrying about how
tired we will be the next day and how that might affect us. We get mentally
exhausted as the anxiety grows; we might become cross or frustrated and
perhaps blame ourselves or others for our sleeplessness. The mindful
approach would be to notice the stories we are telling ourselves (whose
fault it is, the crystal-ball gazing, and so on), acknowledge them, and take our
attention to the body, noticing the breath and the sensation of contact with
the bed and the covers. Every time our thoughts pull us away, the invitation
would be to bring our attention back to the body and remind ourselves
that we can still rest without being asleep.

When we experience physical pain, we often tense up around the
discomfort, thereby creating additional tension elsewhere in the body.

Notice how you brace yourself against a cold wind or as you walk into a room where you anticipate a difficult situation. Every time we do this we are storing up tension in the body, which can have long-term health implications. If we can bring these moments into awareness and soften into the bracing, we are preventing the tension from arising in the first place.

Accepting things as they really are

Our seeing is often clouded by judgments or our mood. By tuning into our experience, we learn to see things as they really are (even when that is not what we want). We spend a lot of time fantasizing about the future or living in the past. It is only by acknowledging where we actually are (rather than where we think we are) that we can move forward.

Creating a personal early warning system

Practicing mindfulness helps us to become more aware of our thoughts, emotions, and physical sensations. It allows us to develop a personal early warning system, alerting us when things are not quite right, such as when we are feeling low or physically unwell. This feedback can help us to take care of ourselves before a situation worsens.

Waking up to life

Although mindfulness can have a therapeutic element, there are other benefits too. It can help us to reconnect with being alive. Many of us operate on automatic pilot. We zone out from an unpleasant commute or dull household chores, for example. However, this can quickly become our default mode of living. When we are on autopilot, we operate from the more primitive parts of the brain and so we are more likely to be reactive, because the higher, executive functions of the brain are not engaged. Since we are not alert, we are also more likely to miss things—both internally (how we are feeling) and externally (our environment and how others are feeling). We are no longer present; it is as if we are sleepwalking through life.

Sensory awareness

When we pay attention to our experience, we become more aware of the senses: taste, smell, touch, sound, and sight. As well as making daily life richer, this can have a major impact on the food we eat. When we eat mindfully, we savor each mouthful, exploring textures and noticing aromas and tastes, and the experience is made richer because of it. Similarly, if the food we are eating is processed, we will notice how it actually tastes, rather than just swallowing it without awareness. This may influence the choices we make going forward. When we eat more slowly and are attuned to the body, we pick up physical cues when we have had enough. Mindfulness brings unconscious behaviors, such as reaching for another cookie or an extra glass of wine, into our awareness so we can make a choice about what we really want.

Being kinder to self and others

People often report being kinder to themselves as a result of practicing mindfulness. Realizing that we are only human with all the associated vulnerabilities can be liberating. Practicing mindfulness regularly has been shown to increase activation in the area of the brain that is linked to compassion and empathy.

Improved focus and attention

Learning to bring our attention back when it wanders is central to meditation practice. Studies have shown that regularly practicing meditation improves focus and concentration. This includes the working memory, essential for reasoning and decision-making, which is degraded by stress.

Seeing the bigger picture

Studies have also shown increased activation in the area of the brain that affects perspective. Most of us spend a lot of time fantasizing about the future or wishing things were as they used to be, or that we could change the past. However, the only opportunity to influence what happens next is to do something different in this moment. Mindfulness helps us to do that by bringing the present moment into our awareness.

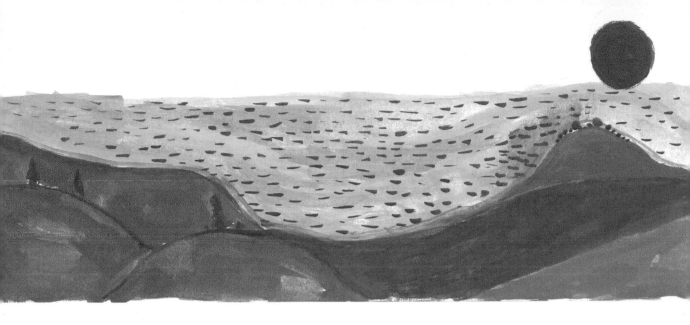

STRESS

All of us will experience stress at some point. Even a positive event, such as a wedding or having a baby, can be stressful. Although stress is often spoken of as a negative thing, we can experience "good" stress—the buzz of doing a performance or delivering a presentation, perhaps. We all need to be stretched intellectually and physically in order to grow and develop, and when this happens without overstretching our resources, we thrive. It can be just as stressful to be under-challenged as overstretched.

The stress reaction

When a threat is perceived, the amygdala (the most primitive part of the brain) activates the alarm, putting the body on high alert. This is called the stress reaction and it is the body's way of keeping us safe. It can only cause problems when it is activated needlessly and repeatedly. Stress hormones, such as cortisol and adrenaline, flood the body, and long-term bodily functions to do with growth, such as digestion and reproduction, shut down so as not to waste valuable resources. Everything is geared toward surviving that moment—the "fight or flight" response. Pupils dilate to improve sight, hairs stand on end to pick up vibrations, the body evacuates

any unnecessary weight so it can run faster (hence the need to go to the toilet), blood is diverted away from the surface of the body in case of wounding, and the heart begins to pound so blood can be pumped faster around the body.

In the meantime, the brain continues to collect additional information about the situation from the senses, memories, and associations to determine if the perceived threat is real. If it isn't, the body stands down and the long-term growth functions resume.

Having butterflies in the stomach is a sign that the digestive system is shutting down.

Chronic stress

If the stress reaction is activated only periodically, there is no harm done. In fact, it is reassuring to know that everything is working as it should. However, if we are feeling stressed all the time, the body is thrown into turmoil: the heart is put under pressure; blood pressure rises; digestion and reproduction may be affected; stress hormones, such as cortisol, can kill off brain cells as well as inhibiting new ones from developing, and keep us stuck in a fearful frame of mind. The more frequently the amygdala is activated, the more sensitive it becomes—thus we get caught in an unhelpful loop of reactivity. This can impact on us physically and mentally in the long term.

Therefore the quicker we can spot the early signs of stress and take action, the better.

Helping ourselves

As well as having an inbuilt stress reaction, the body also has an inbuilt calming response, which slows the heart rate, reduces blood pressure, and restarts the long-term growth functions of the body. One way to activate this deliberately is through practicing mindfulness. Mindfulness will also help us to spot the early warning signs (physical and psychological) that we are under pressure and we can then take wise action.

When we are experiencing chronic stress, we tend to give up things that are seen as optional extras—for example, going out with friends, enjoying a hobby, or attending night school—perhaps because we are physically tired, working late, or continually caught up with family demands. Whatever the reasons, our world becomes narrower and narrower. These activities nourish us and are essential to our well-being, so if you find you have dropped them during a busy period, make a conscious effort to pick them up again.

It is also important to remember that we only have so much in reserve. We can often cope with stress initially but, as time passes, the body becomes

TRY THIS

Here are some helpful activities that may help you cope with stress.

o Do something physical, such as going to the gym or taking a walk, to speed up the dispersal of excess stress hormones.

o Do something that nourishes you mentally, such as a creative task, playing a musical instrument, or learning something new. This is helpful in the moment but also essential on an ongoing basis.

o Spend time outdoors—nature and open spaces can help to bring a much-needed sense of perspective.

o Cry: stress hormones are released through tears, so crying can be helpful.

o Recognize that when we are stressed, we are more likely to fall into unhealthy lifestyle habits, so make a conscious choice to eat healthily and drink wisely.

o Meditate (informally and formally), both in the moment of feeling stressed and also when life is going well, in order to "weave your parachute" and have the necessary skills ready when life throws up obstacles.

o Talk to family and friends.

o Explore ways to support yourself at home or at work.

more vulnerable due to age and the demands placed on it. This is why as we get older we often find ourselves less able to cope with things that previously left us unfazed.

Many of the activities (see pages 68–94) will help you to become familiar with your own early signs of stress—these may be physical or behavioral or even particular thought patterns. The activities also offer opportunities for you to explore what nourishes you, so you can draw on them when you need them and incorporate them regularly into your everyday life.

TEASING APART OUR EXPERIENCE

Head = thoughts
Heart = emotions or feelings
Body = physical sensations

The head, heart, and body are the three strands that make up our experience. Usually we are not aware of them individually—we just know that we are happy, sad, angry, or something else. Our experience feels like a solid blob.

When we practice mindfulness, we are deliberately paying attention to our experience as it unfolds, so that means noticing our thoughts (head), what we are feeling emotionally (heart), and what we are feeling physically (body). We are teasing apart the "blob" of our experience and becoming aware that it is made up of these different elements (and sometimes multiple manifestations within each of these).

The act of breaking down our experience in this way introduces some space into the blob. I like to think of it as teasing apart a knotted tangle of yarn or thread. The knot is solid and any individual colors are lost. But once the knot is teased apart, we can see chinks of light and begin to identify distinctly colored strands of yarn. All the elements that made up the solid knot are still there, but there is space, too, and the knot is no longer solid or tightly bound.

In order to separate the different strands, there has to be an element of curiosity and interest present (see page 40) that characterizes the "approach" mode of mind (see pages 32–33). For example, we may still be feeling angry, but the curiosity that is exploring "anger" creates a sense of witnessing or perspective that may help us to feel less overwhelmed by the anger.

Remember that we may sometimes check in with ourselves and there's nothing in particular to notice, which is okay, and there's no need to go hunting for thoughts or an emotion.

THE LIGHT OF AWARENESS

We explore our experience with our attention, using it like a flashlight. We can direct light onto our inner experience as well as onto the world around us.

The light allows us to see our experience more clearly. Sometimes the flashlight casts a narrow beam, focusing on only a small area. At other times it is wider, illuminating a larger area. Both types of illumination are useful.

We can practice playing with our attention as if it were a beam of light, sometimes making it tightly focused on one thing, such as the breath or sounds or an itch on our nose, and sometimes widening it to include many things: the warmth of the sun on the face, a radio blaring in the background, and the rise and fall of the chest as the breath enters and leaves the body.

It is useful to practice both types of awareness. For example, in Walking Practice (see page 60) we may begin focusing our attention on the soles of the feet. After a few minutes we might expand our awareness to include the whole body, sounds, and other aspects of the world around us, and then we might narrow our focus back to the feet.

TRY THIS

First, become aware of the breath in your chest, feeling the sensations of breathing… and then expand your attention outward, maintaining an awareness of the breath in the chest but also experiencing the feet on the floor, the buttocks on the seat, and perhaps the sensation of the chair at your back. Play with expanding your attention as far outward as you can (like a radar rippling out) and then slowly bring it back in, to focus solely on the breath. Play with this, repeating it several times.

○ ○ ○ ○ ○ ○ ○

THE POWER OF THE BREATH

We use the breath as a vehicle or conduit for our attention. It is a key tool in practicing mindfulness.

The breath is a powerful object to focus on for a number of reasons:

o It is always with us.
o It is always changing. This makes it more interesting and easier to give it our attention.
o It reflects our state of mind and body, so it is a great source of feedback on how we are at any one time.
o It is easy to feel its physical manifestation as it enters and leaves the body (you can place a hand on the belly or chest to help with this).

The breath can act as an anchor—a place to come back to when our attention wanders. Since it is always changing, when we pay attention to it, we are immediately brought into the present moment.

TRY THIS

o Clench your fist really hard for a minute or two. What do you notice?
o Relax the fist and flex your fingers.
o Clench the fist again, but this time imagine you are breathing in and out of the fist. What do you notice this time?

People often report that when they clench their fist in the normal way, they notice other parts of the body tensing up as well and that they are holding their breath. This is what happens to us every time we tense up in our daily life. When we intentionally direct the breath into the clenched fist, there is an overall softening—in the fist and other parts of the body. The breath continues to flow easily. The fist is still clenched but it is not so tight—there is some space in it—and there is less tension elsewhere.

Watching the Breath is a core meditation practice (see page 52). It can be done informally, sitting in the office or in the car or on a train, or more formally, at home or in a quiet place, for a longer period of time. The more often we can watch the breath, the more familiar we become with it (and what is "normal" for us) and the more practiced we become at harnessing its power.

BREATHING INTO

Breathing into describes directing the breath into a particular part of the body. It is a way of tuning into the body (see opposite).

By focusing on the breath and then directing it to a specific place in the body, we are using it as a way of intentionally diverting our attention.

Breathing into has a tight focus, unlike Being With (see page 30), which has a much wider one. It is helpful to be familiar with both and practice them regularly.

TRY THIS

o Become aware of the physical sensations of breathing.

o Now, in your mind's eye, become aware of your right foot. You may not feel anything and that is okay.

o Then, holding both your right foot and your breathing in awareness, imagine that you are breathing directly in and out of your foot.

o Notice if you get caught up in "doing it right." If that happens, just let it go.

o Continue in this way for a couple of minutes.

o Practice doing the same thing with your focus on other areas of the body, such as the whole leg or a single finger.

○ ○ ○ ○ ○ ○ ○

TUNING INTO

Tuning into is another technique of directing our attention in mindfulness practice.

Tune into, or take your attention to, is a phrase we often use in mindfulness practice when we want to become aware of a focus such as the breath, feet on the floor, sounds, and so on, but what does it mean?

Tuning into, or taking your attention to, simply means becoming aware of, and noticing, the felt sensations of the experience, rather than thinking about it.

Take a minute or two now to think about your feet on the floor. What do you notice when you think about your feet? Now, instead of thinking about the feet, explore the sensations of the feet on the floor. Notice any sense of contact: weight, pressure, a sense of shoe or sock, warmth or coolness. Perhaps notice internal sensations, such as a tingling or numbness. Connect with the floor and the earth beneath you.

It really doesn't matter what you discover but the important thing is to experience the felt sensations of feet on the floor. Can you appreciate the difference between thinking about and experiencing the felt sensations? Of course, we often slip between the two and we begin tuning into the felt sensations but get hijacked by thinking about them. This is normal, and we will look at the mind wandering and what to do about it on page 48.

TURNING TOWARD ALL EXPERIENCE

Mindfulness is not about focusing on the positive. It is much more than that. When we practice mindfulness, we are interested in all our experience: the good, the bad, and the neutral.

It is also not about trying to change a neutral or negative experience into a positive one, although that may arise by simply taking a different stance on a difficult experience.

We are not chasing any particular experience either. Whatever arises is worthy of our attention. And when nothing arises, experiencing "nothing" and how that feels in the body and our relationship to it is interesting to explore too.

Turning toward means being interested
in what is arising.

Turning toward suggests a willingness to acknowledge what is present (even when we don't like it and wish it weren't there). Usually when we experience something that we don't like, we try to avoid it. This reaction is normal and plays an important role in keeping us safe. When we practice mindfulness, we are learning to do something different—we learn to turn toward that which we would normally avoid. There are different ways we can do this. One of them is Being With (see page 30), where we use the breath as a container to hold whatever is arising.

When we are willing to be with whatever arises, we are accepting what is present—it is our resistance to our experience that creates most of our suffering. When we stop trying to make things different, we relax.

BEING WITH

We can practice being with when we are meditating and notice something we don't like.

Noticing a physical sensation, such as an itch or a pain, or maybe the physical manifestation of an emotion like sadness, such as a tightness in the chest and a prickle behind the eyes, is the first step.

Then, tiptoe toward the difficulty by acknowledging that things are feeling difficult, perhaps mentally labeling the sensation or emotion: a tight chest, sadness, and so on. Then take your attention to the breath—commonly in the belly or chest but perhaps around the nostrils—and begin to follow the breath entering and leaving the body (see page 52). Take time to ground yourself with the breath or connect with the sensation of your feet on the floor.

When you feel ready, widen your awareness to include any physical sensations of the unpleasant experience. If they are particularly strong or the experience just feels too much, stay with the sensations only very briefly before returning to the breath or your feet on the floor. Stay there or, if it feels okay, tune into the sensations once more, however fleetingly.

TRY THIS

o Taking care of yourself is always the priority.

o Acknowledge what is present.

o Be curious.

o Explore any sensations you can feel in the body.

o When your attention is pulled away (which it will be), just guide it back to the breath and body.

o Use the breath and body as a home base and keep bringing your attention back to them so you are not overwhelmed by whatever may be arising.

o If you feel overwhelmed, stop!

o o o o o o o

In this way, dance back and forth, always using the breath and body as an anchor, a place of safety. It's important to remind ourselves that we are not trying to fix or change the experience, but rather we are practicing being with it as best we can.

Look after yourself

There is no benefit from gritting your teeth and being with a pain or discomfort without any regard for your well-being. You can choose to have 99 percent of your attention on your breath and only 1 percent on the sensation. Dip in and out of it so it does not feel overwhelming. However, if at any time it does feel too much, then just stop. Sometimes it is wiser to avoid something difficult altogether until you are feeling stronger and better able to be with it (see page 45).

THE POWER OF THE BODY

Many of us spend most of our time in our heads, problem-solving our way through life. While this can be effective with practical issues, it is less helpful when it comes to emotional ones.

Trying to think our way out of emotional distress actually works against us, as we get stuck in a never-ending loop of thinking that just perpetuates and exacerbates anxiety. For those predisposed to depression, this type of rumination can tip them into a depressive episode. However, mindfulness teaches us to do something different.

We can tune into the body—the physical sensations arising as a direct result of what we are experiencing. Even if there are no apparent sensations, the act of tuning into the body is what is significant.

We can explore our experience through bodily sensations (or the absence of them). We can be curious about the different sensations arising—what they are like, where they are, and how they are changing moment by moment.

When we do this, we move into an "approach" mode or mind-set, which is characterized by curiosity and openness (activating the left prefrontal cortex). When we are in the approach mode, we are more creative and able to handle difficulties with more equanimity. This is the opposite of the "avoidance" mode or mind-set, characterized by fear, negativity, and worry (activating the right prefrontal cortex).

The body also stores tension and emotions. When we tense up—against an emotion or as a result of our posture—the body stores that tension, and it may become so habitual that it creates long-term problems due to poor posture and alignments. Every time we suppress our feelings, we are just pushing them away so they lie beneath the surface. This can create a pressure-cooker-type feeling.

Tuning into the body mindfully can help us to release stored tension and emotions safely, as long as we are patient and let things unfold in their own time.

Intentionally tuning into the physical manifestations of thoughts and emotions also helps us to explore them in a different way than usual. Practicing curiosity toward unpleasant physical sensations allows us to approach difficulties in a roundabout way that feels more manageable and less overwhelming—provided we do so mindfully (see Turning Toward All Experience, page 28).

Historically it was believed that once we were adult, our ability to handle difficult emotions was fixed—some of us were better able to handle it than others and that was just how it was. However, research has discovered the brain is a lot more plastic than previously thought and change in adulthood is possible. Studies have shown that people who regularly practice mindfulness meditation experience increased activation in the left prefrontal cortex—the area of the brain better able to handle difficult emotions and characterized by the approach mode. This shift from right-sided activation (avoidance mode) to left-sided activation (approach mode) occurred in an eight-week period of practicing mindfulness meditation. Every time we actively turn toward our experience, we reinforce the neural pathways of the approach mode.

NOTICING THE NARRATIVE

Our thoughts drive our actions and behaviors, affecting how we feel physically and emotionally (and vice versa).

Most people are unaware of this thinking process and how it is influencing them, but when we practice mindfulness, we bring it into awareness.

We notice how the type of thoughts we have are influenced by the mood we are in. If we are feeling down, our thoughts will take on a more negative tone than if we are feeling happy. If our interpretation is so easily influenced by our mood, that tells us that our interpretation cannot be assumed to be accurate. Once we realize this, we notice how many of the stories we are creating in our minds are just that: stories—fiction rather than fact.

When we pay attention to our experience as it unfolds, we notice how much we are generating our own suffering. Something negative happens to us but, rather than letting it go, we keep it alive by picking it over and replaying it repeatedly. Each time we do this, the negative story becomes more entrenched. We focus only on what reinforces our story and discount any information that might undermine it.

We notice how often we fuel negative mind-states with a particular story line, perhaps catastrophizing events or overgeneralizing how "this always happens to me…." The more we pay attention, the more we notice how repetitive these stories can be. We become familiar with our own "chart-toppers."

Sometimes we are alerted to the storytelling by the accompanying physical sensations (often unpleasant). With mindfulness, we can tune into the body, bringing an attitude of curiosity to how the narrative manifests itself. As well as shifting us from the head into the body, this creates some perspective as we move from avoidance mode ("I don't like that") to an approach mode of mind ("I'm interested in finding out more") (see pages 32–33).

It is only when we become aware of something that we have the power to do something differently:

o When you notice the narrative galloping away, acknowledge its presence with a gentle, "There I go again...."

o Tune into the body and explore the felt sensations that are associated with a particular narrative.

o Notice the warning signs signaling that your thoughts have become storytelling: perhaps a change in the thought tone, maybe physical sensations or emotions arising. Become familiar with your own red flags.

o When you notice the storytelling mind, remember that it is just a story. As mindfulness expert Professor Mark Williams reminds us, thoughts are not facts (even the ones that say they are).

o Give your chart-topping stories humorous names to create a bit of perspective and help you identify with them less.

CORE ATTITUDES

There are seven core attitudes that are useful to bear in mind as you practice and which will also be cultivated through practice: Beginner's Mind, Non-judging, Kindness, Curiosity, Letting Go of Expectations, Non-striving, and Patience.

BEGINNER'S MIND

Beginner's mind means approaching things as if for the very first time, seeing the world through the eyes of a child with a sense of curiosity and wonder. We drop preconceptions and are willing to be open to whatever arises. It is a "not-knowing" that is rich in potential.

Usually, once we have had an experience, we tend to file it away with the "been there, done that, got the t-shirt" mentality. If we have that experience again, we assume it will be exactly the same but, of course, it never is. It may be better or worse but it is always different. There is the potential for finding out more about ourselves and others, whatever unfolds. This is the richness of life available to us, if we are willing to be open to it.

NON-JUDGING

One of the first things people often notice when they begin practicing mindfulness is how judgmental they are: toward themselves, others, their experience, everything!

Judging our experience usually results in it falling short in some way: we/it/they are not good enough. This makes us feel inadequate and/or disappointed. When we judge something, we are expecting a particular outcome and we usually fail to recognize wider possibilities that may be even better.

Judgment is different from discernment. There is nothing wrong with having a preference for something or someone.

When we notice the judging thought, it is important not to judge ourselves for that as well—it's easy to get caught up in a spiral of judging the judging!

Bringing an attitude of curiosity (see page 40) to what you are experiencing will help shift the mind from avoidance into approach mode (see pages 32–33). Cultivate an attitude of friendly interest in the judgment. Can you feel it in the body? If so, where is it and what does it feel like? Are you aware of the story that is playing out in the mind? Is it a familiar one?

Remember the importance of practicing kindness (see page 38), not only to others but also to yourself.

KINDNESS

Kindness is at the heart of mindfulness practice and it is closely allied with non-judging (see page 37). Becoming kinder to oneself is commonly cited as one of the main benefits of practicing mindfulness. However, you can't just order yourself to be kinder—it is an attitude that arises out of practicing regularly.

> When we practice mindfulness regularly,
> we cultivate a friendly, kindly attitude to
> our experience.

When our mind wanders and we realize it, we can mentally congratulate ourselves for noticing the wandering mind and bring our attention back to the focus without any recrimination.

When we notice thoughts, emotions, or sensations arising that perhaps we don't approve of or think are inappropriate, or that we should be able to put up with, we can simply acknowledge them and remind ourselves that this is our experience and it's okay.

Notice the "thought tone" and whether it sounds harsh or gentle. When you notice the former, acknowledge it with a gentle, "There I go again!"

If you are someone who sets impossibly high standards for yourself, remind yourself that you can only do your best. This will vary depending on the circumstances, but most of the time our best is good enough. It can be helpful to imagine yourself as a close friend in the same situation and then explore your response to them. We often find that we would be kinder to our friend and more supportive of them than we would be to ourselves.

TRY THIS

When you notice you are giving yourself a hard time, it can be helpful to acknowledge it (without judging it) and then place a hand over the chest or perhaps hold both arms (as if you were hugging yourself). Connect with the warmth of the body, perhaps feeling the pulse of the heartbeat, and repeat silently to yourself, "It's okay," as if you were soothing a crying child.

How do you nourish yourself—mentally as well as physically? It can be helpful to notice which activities and people replenish rather than deplete you, and make an intention to do more of those activities and spend more time with those people, particularly when things are difficult and you are feeling stressed.

○ ○ ○ ○ ○ ○ ○ ○ ○ ○

CURIOSITY

When we pay attention to our experience, we encourage an attitude of "friendly interest"—moving in a bit closer, getting to know what is unfolding moment by moment, wanting to explore and discover.

Curiosity assumes a willingness to discover what is present, without any agenda.

We can practice curiosity by asking ourselves, "What is here?" rather than "Why is this here?"

We can become interested in what we are experiencing, particularly physical sensations. Where is it? What does it feel like: stabbing, tingling, throbbing, dull, sharp…? Is it constant or changing? Hard or soft? Does it have a sense of temperature: warm, hot, or cold?

We can be curious about whether a thought has an accompanying emotion or emotions, and any associated physical sensations. Ask questions without any sense of analysis or wanting to know "why." An attitude of warm, friendly curiosity activates the approach mode of mind (see pages 32–33).

LETTING GO OF EXPECTATIONS

When we practice mindfulness, we are practicing letting things unfold in their own time and letting go of particular expectations.

When we have an expectation that something is going to be a particular way, we are closing our mind off to the myriad possible outcomes that we haven't thought of. If we are constantly measuring ourselves or others against some imaginary scale, we are going to be disappointed if we/they fall short and we may blame ourselves or others for this. That disappointment may also cloud our view and make us unable to see any benefits that may have arisen.

When we notice expectations arising, we can remind ourselves to experiment with attitudes of beginner's mind (see page 36) and curiosity (see opposite). Remember not to judge yourself for your expectations. Simply acknowledge them and notice how they may be affecting you. Tune into your head, heart, and body (see page 22).

NON-STRIVING

Striving has a sense of leaning forward toward some better time or place or toward being a better person. It suggests a dissatisfaction with how things are. In that frame of mind we are not present—and if we are always projecting forward, we are never going to arrive in this moment, because when we get there, we will be striving for the next. Yet this moment is the only moment of importance. What we do now, in this moment, affects what happens in the next.

The only way something will change is to do something different in the present moment. Non-striving is about being where we are. Remind yourself that there is nowhere to get to but here right now.

Become familiar with what striving feels like to you. When you are in that frame of mind, how does it feel in the body? Be curious about what you are feeling and where and how it might change from moment to moment. Notice the head, heart, and body (see page 22).

PATIENCE

It is important to remember that our patterns of thinking and behavior have been built up over many years and many thousands of repetitions. Change will take time—and you have a lifetime in which to practice.

Patience is cultivated through meditation. When we feel an impulse arising during meditation—perhaps to scratch an itch or to jump up and stop meditating—we can notice it, acknowledge it, and explore how it feels in the body and mind. We can ride out the impulse, perhaps a few times or maybe just the once. However it is, we are practicing patience and staying with things as they are.

Every time we notice our mind has wandered and every time we bring our attention back to a point of focus, we are laying down new neural pathways in the brain. If we do this just once or twice, it is not going to make any difference to our thinking, but if we do it thousands of times (notice how much your mind wanders every time you meditate), then new patterns of thinking will begin to emerge. If we consciously engage in helpful behaviors—looking after ourselves with exercise, eating healthily, and doing nourishing activities—we will create new habits. All of this takes time, so when you notice that sense of striving (see opposite), acknowledge it and remind yourself that we are all works in progress.

Our practice will go up and down. We will have times when it feels very solid, yet also other times when it becomes a real struggle. This is all part of the process and it is important to hang on in there and just keep going. Often it feels as if we have to learn the same lessons over and over. This is normal.

ABOUT PRACTICE

The more you put into mindfulness, the more you will get out of it. If you want to see long-term change, you do need to practice regularly.

It is better to practice mindfulness a little every day if you can—and the practices and activities in Chapter 2 are designed to support you with that. It is also helpful to do some "formal" meditation on a regular basis, as the skills learned here carry through to the informal practices.

On the following pages, there are instructions for some core practices for you to try, both formally and informally: Watching the Breath (see page 52), Breath and Body (see page 56), Opening to Sounds (see page 58), and Walking Practice (see page 60).

Formal practice

If you are doing a formal practice, choose a place and time where and when you won't be disturbed. See Taking Your Seat, page 46, for advice on how to sit comfortably. Begin with a short practice—perhaps just five minutes or less at first—and build up from there. It is always better to be realistic about what is achievable than be overambitious and disappointed. If you have somewhere you have to be afterward, set an alarm or timer and place it under a cushion so that any sound is muffled.

Informal practice

A number of practices in Chapter 2 refer back to these core meditation practices and you will find it easier to do them on the go if you are familiar with them.

Taking care of yourself

It is important to take care of yourself—if at any time you feel overwhelmed when practicing, please stop. Timing is everything and, in general, it is not recommended that you start to practice if you have been recently bereaved or undergone a major health diagnosis or life event. If you are currently depressed, you may find it challenging to remain motivated. In these circumstances, we recommend you wait until things are on a more even keel. It is better to begin practicing mindfulness when you are feeling well. You can then use the skills you have developed if and when life throws a curve ball your way.

Sometimes meditating can stir things up. We are turning our attention inward and that can bring past hurts and traumas to the surface in the form of tears and sadness. If you experience this, be reassured that it is very common and is the body's way of processing what has previously been suppressed. However, if it feels unmanageable, always talk to family or friends and seek professional help. Remember, too, that if nothing arises, it doesn't mean that you are doing anything wrong!

It is inevitable that some physical discomfort will arise when we practice and there are suggestions on page 50 about how to be with this. Never sit through pain with gritted teeth.

TAKING YOUR SEAT

While there is no need to have your body in any complicated pose when meditating, it is helpful to pay attention to posture.

Sitting

The way you sit can support or hinder your practice. When you are sitting correctly, the body feels aligned and it is reasonably comfortable. If the head is falling forward and the chest is caving in, there will be a sense of contraction and collapse, and sleepiness will quickly follow. On the other hand, when you sit tall, with the lower half of the body grounded and the upper part of the body lifting to the sky, there is a sense of strength and stability. Sitting tall in this way also requires some effort, which helps to keep you alert.

   You can sit on a chair (preferably not an easy chair), or kneel or sit cross-legged on the floor. If you are on the floor, you may want to use cushions, blocks, or books to ensure your hips are higher than your knees. The lower half of the body should feel stable.

Make sure your feet touch the floor when sitting on a chair. If they don't, put a cushion or a book underneath them. Likewise, support your knees with cushions if needed if you are sitting cross-legged on the floor.

If you are meditating for any length of time, your body temperature may drop, so have a blanket or wrap close by.

Standing

Come to a point of balance with both feet flat on the floor. Perhaps take a moment to drop your attention to the soles of the feet and then scan back up through the legs, torso, back of the neck, and out through the crown of the head.

Lying down

Since most of the practices in this book are specifically for doing "on the go," there is an emphasis on sitting or standing. But, if it is better for you, you can also adapt them to lying down, flat on your back with your legs outstretched.

Eyes

Your eyes can be open or closed—this may be influenced by where you are. If your eyes are open, perhaps look down to the floor just in front of you and maintain a soft, unfocused gaze.

Intention

Taking your seat is also about making an intention to meditate and to consciously come into a position to do so. Even when we are practicing informally—perhaps while standing in line or sitting in a meeting—we can still consciously take our seat at the start of the practice.

THE WANDERING MIND

It's a common misconception that when we practice mindfulness meditation, we are trying to empty our mind or stop thinking. This simply isn't possible.

It is the nature of the mind to wander. Just as we can't stop the rain from falling or the sun from shining, we can't stop the mind from wandering. What we can do, however, is learn to bring the attention back when it wanders. This is at the heart of mindfulness practice: bringing our attention back from thinking about the past or future and into the present moment.

Each time the attention wanders it is an opportunity to practice bringing it back. When we do this over and over, hundreds and thousands of times, we are laying down new neural pathways in the brain. We are learning to unhook ourselves from thinking. This is important because when we get caught up in that never-ending cycle of thinking or rumination, we are more likely to become stuck in negative thinking or anxious thoughts. So the quicker we notice this and let go of them, the easier it is to nip unhelpful patterns of thinking in the bud. When we notice the mind wandering, it's important to acknowledge it. We can simply name it "thinking," before bringing the attention back to the breath or other focus.

TRY THIS

A busy mind is a great opportunity to give ourselves an effective mental workout! The more we do this, the more we strengthen these helpful strategies, and the more likely we will find ourselves doing them naturally.

1 Notice the mind has wandered (this arises subconsciously).

2 Acknowledge it (for example, label it as "thinking").

3 Give yourself a mental pat on the back for noticing.

4 Bring your attention back to the focus of the practice.

Repeat over and over again!

We can't just tell ourselves to stop thinking about something, but we can give our attention something else to focus on, tuning into or paying attention to the breath, body, sounds, or some other present-moment experience.

It is important to remember to bring the attention back without judging it. Not judging our experience is a key element of mindfulness—we want to encourage, and be willing to be with, all facets of our experience, even those we don't like or wish we weren't having. We also want to encourage our subconscious to tell us when the mind wanders. If we give ourselves a hard time every time it does, we will inhibit this potentially helpful response.

It is also helpful to notice where our wandering mind is going to—what is pulling us away? This helps us become familiar with the typical stories that regularly arise and we can notice what is number one on today's "hit parade."

PHYSICAL DISCOMFORT

When we practice mindfulness, we are interested in all aspects of experience, including those we normally try to get rid of as quickly as possible, such as physical discomfort.

If we are doing a formal practice, such as Watching the Breath (see page 52), we want to find a position that keeps us alert yet relaxed, so we are not deliberately setting ourselves up to feel uncomfortable. However, if we sit in meditation for any period of time, it is likely that physical discomfort will arise.

The first step is always to acknowledge what is present (itch on the nose, pins and needles, and so on). Then there are different options about how to proceed.

Option 1
We can breathe into the sensation (see page 26).

Option 2
We can use the breath to be with the sensation (see page 30).

Option 3
We can move a little closer to the sensation by getting to know it better. Bring an attitude of curiosity (see page 40) by asking questions such as, "Where exactly am I feeling it?", "How would I describe it?", "Is it hard or soft, constant or changing?" This questioning is with a spirit of exploration, rather than analysis. We are curious about what we are experiencing in this moment—and the next, and the next.

Scratching the itch

We can experiment with any of the above options but at some point we may still make a conscious decision to "scratch the itch." This is okay! However, the suggestion is to do it mindfully: scratch the itch and know you are scratching it! Or move and settle into your new position mindfully.

Trying to fix or making go away

It is important that, regardless of the option you choose, you do not have an underlying aim of getting rid of the sensation. However subtle, such an aim will undermine what happens next. The core paradox with practicing mindfulness is that by accepting things as they are, we relate to our "suffering" differently, with the result that it often feels less overwhelming.

Being kind to yourself

There is nothing to be gained from gritting your teeth in order to bear discomfort or pain. Taking care of yourself, in whatever way works for you, is central to every practice. Staying with an uncomfortable sensation for a fleeting moment is enough to start with—just doing something different and breaking that automatic cycle of reactivity is an important first step. Practicing being with discomfort—for however short a time—flies in the face of our natural reaction. Therefore, every time we do this, we are practicing being with things when they are not as we would like them. By practicing with an inconvenient but harmless itch, we are learning skills that we can then bring into play when life throws up obstacles and challenges.

CORE PRACTICES

The four core meditation practices given here—
Watching the Breath, Breath and Body, Opening to
Sounds, and Walking Practice—can be done formally
or informally.

WATCHING THE BREATH

Following the breath is a core mindfulness practice. The accessibility of the
breath means we can turn to it at any time and, because it is a moving
target, it offers some traction for our attention and we have to work that
bit harder to follow it.

The characteristics of the breath—fast, slow, shallow, or deep—are
influenced by our state of mind, so being familiar with our breath and when
and how it changes is really useful feedback.

Watching the Breath can be done as a formal meditation practice or more
informally when you are out and about.

The Practice

Take your seat (see page 46).

If you are doing this practice informally, you may be standing or sitting in
a public location. When this is the case, taking your seat is about coming
to a place of balance in the body (both feet flat on the floor, for example).

Turn your attention to the body and specifically the breath. Where are you feeling the breath most strongly?

It may be the chest, belly, or around the nostrils or upper lip, but the location itself is immaterial (and it may be different each time). Simply identify the place and make an intention that this is where you are going to place your attention for the duration of the practice.

Begin following the length of each in-breath, noticing the pause where an in-breath turns into an out-breath, and then again into an in-breath. What are you feeling physically? How does an in-breath feel compared to an out-breath? What differences or similarities do you notice?

It can be helpful to place a hand on the belly or chest to connect with the felt sense of the breath entering and leaving the body.

When we do this practice, we are not thinking about the breath, although, of course, that can happen, and when it does, simply acknowledge it and bring your attention gently back to noticing the sensations of breathing. We are not trying to change the breath or breathe in any particular way, but if this happens naturally, just let it be.

Sooner rather than later your mind is going to wander from the breath— perhaps it's thinking about that never-ending to-do list, what you are going to have for dinner, or perhaps how amazing your life will be when you land your dream job/partner/house (delete as applicable!). The wandering mind is part of the practice, and you can read more about it on page 48. The instruction always remains the same: when you "wake up" and notice that your attention has wandered, acknowledge it and simply direct your attention to the breath once more.

This continuous wandering and returning of the mind is at the heart of the practice. Every time you let go of a distraction and come back to the breath, you are strengthening your focus and attention and learning to let go of thoughts, which is an important skill. The breath acts as an anchor and our attention is like the rope attached to it… our attention may drift quite far away, but we can use our awareness of the breath to reel the mind back in when it wanders.

○ ○ ○ ○ ○ ○ ○ ○ ○ ○ ○

Settle into the felt sense of breathing, noticing how it comes and goes. Allow the breath to breathe itself.

Continue for a designated period. If you are doing this as a formal practice, it can be helpful to gradually build up the length of time. Perhaps start with five minutes and go from there. The more frequently we do this practice, the more familiar we become with our own patterns of breathing and how it is affected by our state of mind.

Sometimes people find focusing on the breath a bit tricky, perhaps as a result of breathing problems in the past. If this happens to you, let go of the breath and take your attention to the soles of your feet on the floor. Explore that felt sense of contact, rather than the breath, and when the mind goes for a walk, just bring it back to your feet as soon as you notice.

BREATH AND BODY

The Breath and Body meditation is an extension of Watching the Breath (see page 52). It is not a more advanced practice but simply a different one with a varying focus.

The Practice

Take your seat (see page 46). Begin paying attention to your breath (see page 52).

After a while widen your awareness to include the whole body—there will still be an awareness of the physical sensations of breathing (a bit like a radio playing in the background) but also of external sensations—perhaps the weight and contact of your buttocks on the seat, maybe a sense of a draft of air or an itch on your nose—and internal sensations: a rumbling stomach, tight shoulders, a sore throat...

When you become aware of a sensation, be curious about it. Where exactly are you experiencing it? How would you describe it? Does it come and go?

soft... hard... sharp...
tingly... stabbing... throbbing...
fuzzy... spiky... fizzing...
intermittent... constant...
tight... stiff... loose...

○ ○ ○ ○ ○ ○ ○ ○ ○ ○

We are interested in what we are experiencing rather than why. If you experience strong physical sensations, see page 50. We are not trying to change or get rid of any sensation. We are practicing allowing it to be there (since it already is). Sometimes we may need to adjust our position or "scratch the itch" and that's okay. We acknowledge its presence and make a conscious decision to scratch it. This is very different from the usual unconscious itching that we do to relieve a discomfort and make it go away.

OPENING TO SOUNDS

We can't always control the sounds around us, and although some may be pleasant, there will probably be some that are not.

Drilling outside your window, a noisy neighbor's constant partying... whatever the reason, unwanted noise can have a detrimental effect on us physically and mentally. But it is often the story we create around the noise that causes more suffering than the noise itself. Making sounds the focus in meditation is one way we can practice being with all sounds—that is, changing our relationship to them so we can allow them to be there—even the ones we don't like.

The Practice

Take your seat (see page 46). Spend a few minutes watching the breath and body (see pages 52–57). Then widen your awareness to include sounds—any sounds—that come your way.

They may be far away or perhaps close by, or even internal sounds from within the body. There is no need to hunt for them but simply allow the body to pick up and receive sounds as if it were a radar.

○ ○ ○ ○ ○ ○ ○ ○ ○ ○

Notice when a sound is judged good, bad, or neutral. Be curious about how sound affects you in the body—perhaps making you start or wince, or even experience an overall softening.

Notice when you begin to create a story about a sound—and also notice the accompanying physical manifestations of that narrative.

It doesn't matter what the story is but as soon as you notice it, acknowledge it and let it go.

You can do this by becoming curious about how the story manifests itself in the body and exploring those sensations. At some point, widen your awareness once more to receive sounds. Sometimes it can be helpful to narrow your awareness onto the breath for a moment or two before widening it out.

Continue practicing in this way. To finish, bring your attention back to the breath once more.

Opening to Sounds as a practice can be done inside or outside for a minute or two or as an extended sitting practice. Sitting on a park bench or in a busy café will be very different experiences. Sometimes the emphasis may be on pleasing sounds and at other times the opposite. Remember that we are not trying to have a particular experience or turn something we don't like into something pleasant. We are simply learning to be with all experiences.

○ ○ ○ ○ ○ ○ ○ ○ ○ ○ ○

WALKING PRACTICE

Walking as meditation is a great way to integrate mindfulness into your daily life and is particularly helpful if sitting feels too challenging.

The instruction is simple: *walk and know that you are walking.*

You can do the practice inside or out. You only need an area of just over a yard or about a meter around you, and you can walk back and forth in a straight line or around in a circle. Whether you're walking slowly or normally, whenever the mind wanders, just bring it back (see page 48).

Walking slowly

If you are doing the practice in a place where you won't feel self-conscious, you can walk slowly. We do this to remind ourselves that we are walking in a different way than usual—without the need to get from A to B—and simply walking for its own sake. Slowing down the process gives us a chance to break the action down into micro movements—lifting, shifting, and placing the feet—and to notice how different parts of the body become involved at every stage.

From time to time, you can widen your awareness to include the whole body and the environment (sounds, scents, the sun or rain on your skin) but then narrow it back down again. Notice what happens to your attention when the focus is wider or narrower.

○ ○ ○ ○ ○ ○ ○ ○ ○ ○

You may want to experiment with taking your
shoes off to increase the sense of contact
and feel the subtle movements of the
foot as it takes each step.

Walking normally

Here you are walking at your normal pace, so the challenge is to avoid
falling into habitual patterns. You won't have much time to focus on points
of contact, so keep the awareness wider—on the body as it moves through
space and on the environment around you.

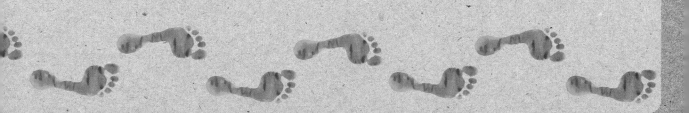

chapter 2

activities and practices

ABOUT THE ACTIVITIES AND PRACTICES

There are **26** activities and **26** practices. The activities (see pages **68–94**) focus on becoming aware of your habitual patterns of behavior, as well as ways that mindfulness can help you to cultivate new ones. The practices (see pages **95–121**) are mini meditations to do while you are out and about.

What to do when

There are many ways to introduce mindfulness into your daily life but it can be overwhelming to know what to do when, and so you may end up doing nothing. This book solves that problem for you. All you have to do is pick a random page from this chapter and follow the instructions for the day. Just focus on that single practice or activity. This will help you to remember to do it throughout the day, while the repetition of the practice or activity will help to embed it in your memory so it will be available to you in the future.

   You can pick an activity or practice every day, or just from time to time. However, research suggests that practicing little and often is the most helpful at effecting change. Every time we do something different, we are laying down neural pathways in the brain—changing the brain and how it works—so the more we do it, the quicker this will happen.

I recommend you limit yourself to one activity or practice per day. As time goes on, you may find yourself doing some of the practices spontaneously, and that is fine (and what this book is designed to cultivate).

It is also helpful to reflect on what you noticed at the end of the day—encouraging an attitude of curiosity.

Just do it

Another benefit of choosing a random practice is doing what it suggests, regardless of whether you want to. We all have a tendency to focus on activities that we like or are "good at." However, it is always beneficial to do something regardless of how we feel about it. Adopting this approach will encourage us to do the same in other areas of our life where we often have to do or face things that we would rather not.

If you come across an activity or practice that doesn't appeal to you or seem relevant, I would encourage you to notice what is going on. What thoughts are arising? What are you feeling in your body? And, if possible, still do the exercise even if you don't want to, and thereby experiment with things not being as you would like them to be.

The power of intention

Setting a clear intention at the start of the day (or whenever you choose an activity or practice) is a really helpful way to support your practice. Therefore, once you have chosen one, take a moment or two to read it, making sure you are clear about what is being asked of you and then make a definite intention to do whatever is suggested as best you can. "As best you can" is important! See pages 36–43 for helpful attitudes to support your practice.

Making the most of time

People often complain that they don't have time to practice mindfulness. Most of the practices in this chapter are simply encouraging you to do what you are doing anyway but to do it in a different way—that is, being aware of what you are doing as you are doing it (and without judging it).

The activities and practices also make the most of those "dead" spaces in our day, such as walking to the store or a meeting, or going up or downstairs. Transitional moments like these are the perfect opportunity for practicing, and no extra time is required.

Many of the activities and practices are kept deliberately short, requiring a few minutes only, but there are longer practices too. Both types can be equally challenging!

REMEMBER

o Try not to cherry-pick favorite exercises (but notice if you do!).
o Bring the core attitudes (see pages 36–43) to any practice or activity.
o Always take care of yourself (see page 45). If at any time you feel overwhelmed, then just stop practicing. If you feel overwhelmed but are interested in continuing, I recommend working with an experienced teacher.
o It's better to take "baby steps" and experiment with moving forward slowly at a pace that feels okay for you.

o o o o o o o

THE ACTIVITIES

1 banking the good   69

2 appreciating the good   70

3 good news   71

4 smiling inside   72

5 random act of kindness   73

6 how do you treat others?   74

7 how do you treat yourself?   75

8 how can I best take care of myself?   76

9 the power of intention   77

10 what is your intention?   78

11 just one thing   79

12 create some space   80

13 willing to be a beginner?   81

14 be a tourist   82

15 do something different   83

16 practice curiosity   84

17 taking a different perspective   85

18 back from the future   86

19 in service to others   87

20 noticing the unpleasant   88

21 what pushes your buttons today?   89

22 what does stress feel like?   90

23 what helps when you   91
    are stressed?

24 how do you behave when   92
    you are stressed?

25 social media: noticing the impulse   93

26 technology detox   94

banking the good

Today, pay attention to any moment that feels good or positive.

What do you notice?
- **Thoughts?**
- **Emotions?**
- **Physical sensations?**

Savor and acknowledge your experience on each occasion, however fleeting.

At the end of the day, reflect back on your experience.

How do you feel now?

Unlike potential threats, there is no survival benefit to remembering pleasant experiences, therefore our default setting is to forget them.

However, if we can savor the moment, pausing to notice how it feels in the head, heart, and body, we can bank it in our long-term memory. We can then bring it out and experience it again whenever we want.

appreciating the good

Friends, family, well-being, freedom from
something difficult, an activity you enjoy, the
scent of a flower, or the smell of newly baked
bread… the taste of something delicious, a roof
over your head, clean water to drink, a job well done…

Name five things you appreciate in this moment.

1 ....
2 ....
3 ....
4 ....
5 ....

It's easy to forget how much is good in our lives. From sharing
a joke with friends, to enjoying the first cup of tea or coffee of
the day, to appreciating our health (even if it is not as good as
we would like), there are always some good things present, even
in the darker times.

good news

The media focuses on drama, death, and destruction, but today, make your focus good news only.

These events might be small milestones, such as a ripening of a long-awaited homegrown tomato, a dog that was lost now found… it doesn't matter what, as long as you perceive it as good news!

Reflect at the end of the day on what you notice:
- in your head
- in your heart
- in your body.

We usually focus on what is wrong and the constant negativity of the media can drag down our mood. Counterbalance this by noticing our own good news stories that are happening in our neighborhood and workplace, to family, friends, and coworkers. Celebrate what is right with us and those we care about.

smiling inside

Pay attention to your face when you smile.

What happens around the mouth and the eyes?
How do you feel inside—perhaps lighter, softer?

Practice smiling internally—a soft, relaxed smile…

How does it make you feel?
What do you notice in others?

Experiments have shown that when two groups watched the same cartoons, with one group holding a pencil in the mouth in such a way as to activate the smiling muscles, the other holding a pencil to activate the frowning muscles, the former rated the cartoons funnier than the latter. Explore for yourself the strong link between the body and emotions.

random act of kindness

Do a random act of kindness for a stranger or a person you know.

It could be as simple as holding a door open for someone struggling with bags, helping someone with a task, giving up your seat on the train…

Act without any expectation of a "reward."

What do you notice?

When we do an act of kindness for someone else, it makes us feel good. Of course, that should not be the motivation for the practice, but it's a nice perk!

how do you treat others?

Notice how you behave toward other people, and notice if there is an internal commentary on how they look and behave.

When you notice any, acknowledge it (even if you don't like what you are thinking or think it inappropriate).

Notice if you judge yourself for judging others. If you do, acknowledge and let it go.

When we bring the judging mind into awareness, we may discover all kinds of biases that we were unaware of. We can't do anything different until we are aware of them, so the first step is always noticing and acknowledging what is present.

7 ACTIVITIES

○○○○○○○○○○○○○○○○○○○○○○○○○○○○

how do you treat yourself?

Notice how you behave toward yourself when you do something good, or when you perhaps make a mistake or do something you regret.

What tone is the internal commentary?
- Friendly?
- Harsh?
- Forgiving?

There's no need to judge, simply acknowledge.

Awareness highlights self-judgment. Once we are aware of it, then we bring an attitude of gentle kindness to it: "Ah, there I go again!"

Human beings make mistakes. We can learn from our mistakes but there's no need to hang onto them or beat ourselves up about them. Practice being kind to yourself.

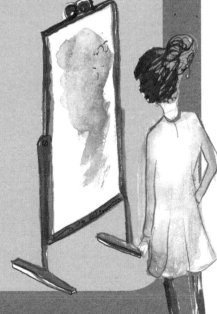

how can I best take care of myself?

Explore how you can nourish yourself physically and mentally.

Notice the choices you make and where you are placing your attention.

Keep asking yourself, "How can I best take care of myself right now?"

Go for a walk, phone a friend, or take a nap. Read a book, listen to music, plant some seeds…

Many of us are better at taking care of others than ourselves. If we can deliberately integrate nourishing activities and choices into our day, we will be constantly nourishing ourselves. Small things can have a much bigger impact than you might think.

the power of intention

Choose an intention for the day:

• to be kinder to yourself or kinder to others

• to open to the present moment

• to slow down

• to notice where your attention is.

Alternatively, make up your own intention.

You will forget the intention, but you will also remember you have forgotten—that is your chance to recommit and, if possible, fulfill the intention right then.

Reflect at the end of the day.

Intentions influence our actions, and setting specific intentions reminds us where we would like to be heading. The constant forgetting and remembering provide an opportunity to recommit to the intention, rather than judge ourselves for forgetting, thereby cultivating kindness as well as intention.

what is your intention?

Notice what is driving your actions today.

Are your intentions:
- **positive?**
- **self-serving?**
- **something else?**

Become aware of thoughts, and notice how you are feeling emotionally and what is arising in the body.

Explore opportunities to cultivate positive intent in your relationships.

Whether our intention is positive, negative, or neutral, it will influence our body language as well as the words we use. How we engage with others will affect how they respond. We can deliberately cultivate a positive intent that will affect how people feel about themselves as well as toward us.

just one thing

Focus on just one thing at a time, making sure you give it your undivided attention.

Notice how doing so affects you and also the job in hand. Experiment with different types of tasks, perhaps while you're at work, out shopping, when you are with other people.

What do you notice?

Multitasking is often praised yet it divides attention. This lack of focus is more inefficient because things are missed, and time and energy are lost due to the constant switching back and forth. Continually bringing your attention back to one point helps to develop concentration and focus.

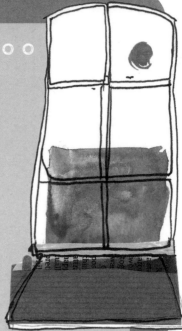

create some space

Deliberately create some space in your day for you alone.

It may be 5 minutes or 60 minutes. However long it is, leave it unplanned and respond to whatever arises in that period.

Notice how it feels before, during, and after.

We can fill our days with activities and things to do. When we are busy, we don't have time to pay attention to how we are. If we can consciously create some unscheduled space, we have the opportunity for the unexpected to arise.

If this feels uncomfortable at first, notice, acknowledge, and stay with it if you can.

willing to be a beginner?

Where could you practice being a beginner in your life today?

What don't you know how to do? Bake a cake? Create a spreadsheet? Run? Ride a bike? Speak some words in a different language? Knit? Sow some seeds? Learn a musical instrument?

A beginner has no expectations of getting it right. A beginner is willing to experiment—to explore what works and what does not—and has no "expert" position to protect. For a beginner there are myriad possibilities.

A beginner is willing to be vulnerable and ask for help. A beginner has the potential to grow and learn.

be a tourist

Imagine you have never visited your hometown or city before.

What would you do differently?

Imagine you don't know your way around:

What would you visit?
Where would you eat?
What would you want to see?

In whatever way you can, be a tourist where you live. Explore. Notice.

When we visit somewhere new, we are alert—finding our way, looking up as well as around in case we miss something. We may stop to take in the view or linger, say, in the market. We notice smells and scents, try local specialties. Perhaps we slip into a church or museum to see a work of art.

Being a tourist wakes us up to our everyday environment.

do something different

Shake things up and do as many things as possible differently.

How many things can you do differently today?

Try a different:

• route...
• choice...
• time...
• place...

Following habitual patterns of behavior demands less of us because we are removing the decision-making process. However, the downside is that we are operating from the more primitive, automatic areas of the brain. We can sleepwalk through much of our day.

When we shake things up, we pay attention, we see more, and we discover things.

We wake up.

practice curiosity

Shine a lamp on your experience as it unfolds, onto the world around you, people you come across, the weather…

Explore without an agenda:

- learn
- discover
- get to know
- be interested and inquisitive.

What do you notice?

What do you discover?

Children are curious about everything but as adults we can lose that quality. Being curious about our experience is integral to mindfulness (see page 40), so it can be helpful to reacquaint ourselves with our childhood curiosity. As always, approach this practice without any specific expectations.

taking a different perspective

Practice seeing the world through someone else's eyes: the official making life difficult but who is hemmed in by regulations, or the person holding up the line chatting to the store assistant—the only person they might talk to today…

Step out of your shoes and into someone else's. Imagine what it must be like.

Explore how that affects you in the head, heart, and body.

We can get stuck at always seeing things from one particular viewpoint—our own, which is inevitably filtered through our own experiences and biases. Regularly practicing mindfulness meditation increases activation in the area of the brain that is linked to perspective.

back from the future

Notice when your thoughts turn to, "If only…"

If only I had a different job/boss/partner…
If only I had more money/time/space…

Notice the thought and what, if anything, precedes it.

Acknowledge and explore the felt sense in the body, along with any accompanying emotions.

If we are constantly fantasizing about a time when all will be wonderful, we are failing to be present in this moment. Continually leaning forward robs us of living now and increases dissatisfaction.

However our life might be, we can only begin to change it if we are actually present in it and know where we are right now.

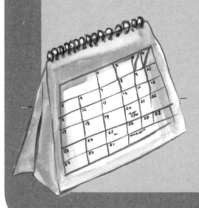

in service to others

Notice the chores you don't like doing.

Perhaps it's the dishes, cleaning, or something else. We can do these activities reluctantly, even resentfully, often zoning out, or we can acknowledge that by doing them we are serving others: our partners, children, friends, neighbors.

What do you notice?

How do you usually do chores that you don't enjoy? Is there a sense of reluctance? Perhaps you wait until someone nags you to do it.

What happens if you make a conscious choice to do the activity—what do you notice? Choosing to do something or not is very empowering and if we choose to do something we don't want to do, it often gives us a positive feeling about the action, even if the activity is still unpleasant. Try it and see.

noticing the unpleasant

Notice when you recoil, turn away, resist your experience.

Become aware of the moment when you react to something you don't like.

There's no need to judge the reaction.

Simply notice how it manifests in:
• the head
• the heart
• the body.

Habitually we tune out from the unpleasant, which means we become used to tuning out all our experience—the good as well as the bad.

Be curious about what makes up "unpleasant" but remember to take care of yourself (see page 45). Explore without any agenda of wanting things to be different.

what pushes your buttons today?

It might be someone cutting in front of you in traffic, a pressing deadline, or a feeling of being overwhelmed. It might be to do with someone else or perhaps it's the eternal to-do list running through your mind. It may be one thing or a lot of things.

Notice:

- who
- what
- when.

There's no need to worry about why.

Noticing what makes us stressed can help us to develop strategies to manage situations. There are always going to be things that are out of our control but simple changes in behavior can sometimes make a difference. Realizing how much we create our own stress empowers us to take action to reduce it.

what does stress feel like?

How does it feel physically when you are stressed?

Butterflies in the stomach? Dry mouth? Or do you experience headaches or stiffness in the body, such as the neck or shoulders? Sometimes becoming aware of an unconscious gesture, such as rubbing an area of the body, can give us a clue.

Tune into the body and name what is present—for example, "clenched jaw."

Bringing an attitude of friendly interest to our experience immediately brings some distance and perspective to what we are experiencing. Make an intention to consciously notice what it feels like when you are stressed. It may feel counterintuitive to explore unpleasant sensations, so treat yourself gently. Notice if there are some sensations that arise ahead of others.

Becoming familiar with our body's specific stress signals will help to create our own early warning system. The more you can tune into this, the better.

what helps when you are stressed?

Experiment and discover activities to support yourself when things are difficult.

Look for things that you can do in the moment and don't require planning, such as phoning a friend, going for a walk or doing other exercise, listening to music, gardening, cleaning, or making something.

Notice what is helpful for you.

It is useful to know what we can do in the moment when we are feeling stressed so that we can turn off the stress reaction and activate the calming response (see pages 17–21).

This will be different for each of us, so creating your own list to draw on when needed is useful.

how do you behave when you are stressed?

Pay attention to what you do when you are stressed, upset, or anxious.

Do you eat more or eat less? Perhaps you make unhealthy choices.
Is your sleep affected?
Do you get more irritable with other people or perhaps yourself?

We are all different so be as specific as you can and notice as many behavioral changes as you can.

Everyone experiences stress from time to time. It is the body responding to whatever challenge is arising (see page 17). The danger is that we get locked into a never-ending stress reaction that impacts negatively on our well-being. Becoming familiar with any changed behavior will help you pick up early warning signs and take wise action.

social media: noticing the impulse

Notice the impulse to access social media.

• What is on your mind?

• What is your mood?

• Are you aware of any physical sensations?

Explore the moment of impulse without judging.

Then, become familiar with the impulse—perhaps noticing what comes before it and whether there are any patterns.

Notice how frequently you access social media.

• Is it automatic and unconscious?

• How does it make you feel?

There is no right or wrong answer. Notice if this varies according to your mood.

Simply bring the moment of impulse into awareness.

technology detox

Give yourself a break and disconnect from your devices for an hour, half a day, or longer; no emails, no social media, no texting…

How does that prospect feel?

The more you resist, the more helpful it will be.

Start with shorter periods and choose times when you will benefit from focusing on what you are doing, such as being with friends and family or doing a pleasurable activity.

Technology is there to support us but it is easy to fall into unhelpful patterns of how we use it. The healthier the relationship you have with your devices, the easier it will be to do this activity. If you find the practice difficult, you probably need to do it!

THE PRACTICES

1   exploring the senses: sight   96
2   exploring the senses: smell   97
3   exploring the senses: sounds   98
4   exploring the senses: taste   99
5   exploring the senses: touch   100
6   eat something you don't like   101
7   acknowledging what is: body   102
8   acknowledging what is: head   103
9   acknowledging what is: heart   104
10 standing like a mountain   105
11 walk, knowing that you   106
       are walking
12 connecting to the earth   107
13 coming into the body   108

14 outlining the body   109
15 tuning into the body posture   110
16 breath awareness   111
17 taking a breathing space   112
18 counting the breath   113
19 just a minute   114
20 letting go   115
21 five plus five   116
22 being with others   117
23 letting things unfold   118
24 practicing self-compassion   119
25 stop on red   120
26 the gift of silence   121

exploring the senses: sight

Go on a vision quest.

• Look up, look down, and look around.

• Stop and stare.

• Get up close and notice.

What do you discover?

When we look, we see things—it sounds obvious but for much of the time our gaze travels over the vista without actually seeing... we tune out from our environment. We rarely look above or below our line of sight and so we miss a huge amount.

We don't notice the richness of colors, textures, and patterns. We might miss some action or activity that is going on. We are effectively sleep-walking.

Of course, we don't always have time to slow down and look, but we can choose to do it when we can. If you are out for a walk, look around you. If you are sitting on a bus or train or at a traffic light, take a moment or two just to look and see what is in front of you, rather than traveling to some distant place in your mind. What is here right now?

2 PRACTICE

exploring the senses: smell

Explore smells and scents—those that waft your way and those you deliberately engage with. Bury your nose in some herbs, breathe deeply next to an overflowing garbage can...

Notice the judgment of good, bad, and indifferent.

- How can you tell the difference?
- What happens in the body?
- What thoughts arise?
- What emotions?

By connecting with smell, we rediscover a sensory awareness. We notice how the heart, mind, and body respond, according to how we judge it. Engaging the senses is a really quick way to shift out of "doing" mode and into "being"—being in the present moment.

Smells are powerful. We may notice how a particular smell might immediately take us back to a particular memory—good or bad—and often we aren't aware that the smell was the trigger.

exploring the senses: sounds

Pay attention to sounds, receiving whatever comes along.

The body is like a receiver of notes. Notice when there is a physical response: a start, a softening of the body, or perhaps an emotion triggered by a memory.

Notice any stories you create about the sound.
Can you let go of them?

The source of our suffering is often the story we create about the sound, for example, the noisy neighbors keeping us awake and wondering how we will cope the next day…

We can't do anything about the "noise," but we can practice letting go of the story and coming back to the body's response.

exploring the senses: taste

Pay attention to the first bite (or sip) whenever anything passes your lips.

Notice the moment it touches the lips.

How does the body respond?

Hold the food momentarily in the mouth, experiencing the texture and shape. Consciously decide when to chew, and then swallow.

What do you notice?

When we place our attention fully on the experience of eating (or drinking), we savor it, noticing texture, sound, smell, and taste. The experience is richer (if we like it) and so we feel more satisfied. By slowing down, we notice the body's cues for when we are full.

exploring the senses: touch

Notice random points of contact, deliberately running your fingers over different surfaces and textures. Notice how textures might be affected by temperature. A soft, furry blanket may feel pleasant when you are cold, but if your hands are warm and sweaty it might be the opposite.

Notice those you like and those you don't.

- How can you tell the difference?
- What happens in the body?
- What thoughts arise?
- What emotions?

By connecting with touch, we rediscover a sensory awareness. We notice how the heart, mind, and body respond differently. Engaging with a touch is an easy and unobtrusive way to connect to this moment, helping us shift out of the head where we are often stuck in the past or leaning forward to the future. If you are feeling a bit nervous, for example, consciously taking your attention to your hands in contact with your lap might be helpful. Sometimes, making a small, discreet movement, such as moving a finger, slowly heightens that sense of touch and connection.

PRACTICE

eat something you don't like

Notice what story is arising before you begin. Then, paying attention to head, heart, and body, take a bite.

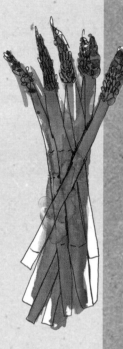

Be curious about the period prior to eating, while eating, and then immediately afterward. Stop eating after one bite if you wish.

What do you discover? There is no expectation that you will change your opinion.

Here we are exploring a willingness to eat something we would normally avoid—and paying close attention to the experience as we do so.

Often we have to do things we would rather not. Practicing turning toward with something like food is great training.

acknowledging what is: body

What body sensations do you notice?

• **Air brushing the skin?**

• **A sense of contact with the floor or seat?**

• **Internal sensations, such as tingling or itching?**

Scan the body tip to toe and back again. What is here? Is there a sense of liking or not liking? Or perhaps neither?

Intentionally scanning the body is a way of exploring what is arising. We may not be aware of any sensations but it is the act of tuning in that is important. By doing this, we become familiar with how the body responds physically to our different moods. We may notice the body more accurately reflects how we feel than we previously thought.

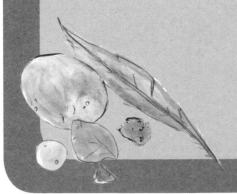

acknowledging what is: head

What is on your mind right now?

• Your to-do list?

• Planning a vacation?

• Going over a conversation?

What story is being created? How does it feel physically and emotionally when you connect with that story?

Acknowledge what is here and then bring your attention to your breath, following it for a few rounds.

We spend most of our time in our head yet without awareness of what is driving our behavior. However, we can practice noticing thoughts. They can give us useful feedback about what is on our mind.

Use the breath as a way to stay in the body and the present moment (see pages 52–57).

9 PRACTICE

acknowledging what is: heart

What are you experiencing emotionally right now? Check in and see what emotions are present.

Acknowledge whatever you discover: irritation is here, relief is here, frustration is here...

Is there a physical manifestation? If so, where and what is it like? Have you created a narrative around what you are feeling emotionally? Notice and acknowledge.

We can become disconnected with what we are experiencing emotionally. By checking in periodically and acknowledging what we are feeling—whether positive, negative, or neutral—and how this manifests itself physically along with any narrative, is a useful practice. We also discover how our emotions are always changing, just like the weather.

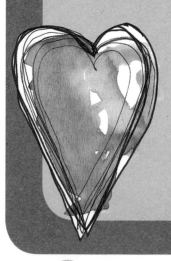

standing like a mountain

Stand tall.

With both feet flat on the floor, run your attention from the base of the spine, up the back of the neck, and out through the crown of the head.

With the lower half of the body grounded, stand with the torso and head lifting to the sky.

Stand like a mountain.

Mountains command a wide perspective and presence. Their outer surface may change radically with the seasons and bear the brunt of the weather, but the essence of the mountain remains. We can borrow those qualities: by standing like a mountain we can meet whatever weather comes our way.

walk, knowing that you are walking

Drop your attention down to the soles of the feet as they lift, shift, and place. Bring the mind back when it wanders.

Experiment:
• Switch between focusing on the feet to expanding out to include the whole body and the environment.
• Walk normally and at other times slowly.

What do you notice?

Walking practice is a great way to weave mindfulness into your everyday life. There are so many opportunities for practice when we are walking outside and also indoors. You can do it for a few steps or take a mindful walk.

Any practice involving movement is also good to do when you are feeling anxious and it is too challenging to stay still.

12 PRACTICE

connecting to the earth

Periodically drop your attention to the soles of the feet.

Notice the sense of contact.
Notice the pressure and weight.
Become aware of any warmth or coolness or other sensations.

Imagine you are breathing in and out through the soles of the feet.

This is a simple way to shift attention from the head (where we may get caught up in unhelpful cycles of thinking) to the body and so ground ourselves with the earth beneath us.

Practice this often, so that when things are tricky, you start doing the practice spontaneously.

coming into the body

Tune into the right side of the body and then the left side.

Become aware of the entire body.

Tune into the lower half of the body and then the top half.

Become aware of the entire body.

Tune into the front of the body and then the back.

Become aware of the entire body.

This practice teaches you to tune into specific parts of the body and then the whole, narrowing and widening your attention. The order of the practice doesn't matter.

There is no expectation that you will feel anything.

outlining the body

Whether standing or sitting, imagine in your mind's eye that you are drawing an outline around the body.

Moving slowly, starting with the feet, move your attention along all the outer and inner edges of the body.

Then, run your attention across and around the contours of the body.

There is no wrong way to do this. All we are doing is bringing our attention to the body, scanning around the shape it makes in the space that it occupies.

Regularly tuning into the body reacquaints us with it and takes us out of the head, bringing us into the present moment.

tuning into the body posture

Standing or sitting, tune into the body.

- Where are your shoulders?
- What about your chin?
- What do you notice about your jaw?
- How about the forehead and between the eyebrows?
- Are the lips soft or pursed tightly?

Pay attention to any parts where you habitually hold stress: the shoulders, jaw, and forehead.

There are links between how we feel in the body with how we feel emotionally, so becoming aware of sensations in the body as an early warning sign is useful.

When we bring an area of tension into awareness, it may soften—the shoulders drop, the frown disappears—but remember that we are not setting out to change our experience.

16 PRACTICE

breath awareness

Tune into your breath.

• Is it fast or slow?

• Long and deep, or short and shallow?

• Does it vary?

Simply become aware of your breath right now. There is no need to change it or breathe in any particular way. When the mind wanders, just bring the attention back to the breath.

Do this for a few minutes at least once.

The breath gives us feedback about how we are right now. Practice tuning in as regularly as you can—little and often is more effective than an occasional longer session.

For further instructions, see Taking Your Seat, page 46; The Power of the Breath, page 24; and The Wandering Mind, page 48.

17 PRACTICE

taking a breathing space

Step 1: Check in to your head, heart, and body. Acknowledge whatever is present, even if you don't like it.

Step 2: Narrow your attention and follow the breath.

Step 3: Widen your attention, becoming aware of the body and what is around you.

Aim to do this three times today or whenever you remember.

This is an opportunity to acknowledge what is present in a particular moment, so it is important not to skip Step 1. Acknowledging is a way of turning toward the "approach," rather than the "avoidance," mode of mind (see pages 32–33).

Step 2 can take as long or as little time as you wish.

You are practicing narrowing and widening your attention (see page 23).

counting the breath

Become aware of the breath and begin counting silently.

Breathing in... breathing out is **1**.

Breathing in... breathing out is **2**.

Continue up to 10. If you lose your place, simply return to 1.

Do 2–3 rounds, depending on the time available.

Counting each breath is a way to support the attention. Your mind will still wander and you will lose count. Starting again is at the heart of all practice.

Do this when you are out and about, or as a longer meditation when you are sitting quietly.

Counting breaths is also a helpful practice if you are lying awake and unable to sleep. Focusing on the breath and body will help shift your attention from the mind, and the counting gives you a bit of focus.

just a minute

You will need a timer in the first instance to measure a minute. Sit with the timer ready and begin watching the breath. Practice counting each in-breath and out-breath as one.

When you are ready, start the timer and begin counting. After 60 seconds, stop.

How many breaths have you taken?

Periodically tune into your breathing for that number of breaths.

The number of breaths you take in the period is irrelevant, because the exercise is just to give you a figure for using subsequently. Once you know how many breaths you take in 60 seconds, take a mindful minute as often as you can.

letting go

Pay attention to the out-breath—the exhalation of air from the body. There's no need to force it or change it in any way. Simply become aware of it.

Notice how the body responds physically.
What do you discover?

Continue to do this practice at different times of the day, whenever you remember.

The out-breath is a perfect example of letting go, of the body softening as it empties of air. You may notice other areas of the body—the shoulders, neck, or face—softening at the same time.

five plus five

Tune into your breathing for five breaths.

Tune into five different parts of the body in turn, being as specific as you can.

Perhaps:

• leg, hand, thumb, big toe, nose.

Or maybe:

• right ear, throat, crown of the head, left ear, lips.

Choose which parts and the order you do them in. Stay with each part for a minute or so.

This versatile and short body scan meditation focuses on just five areas and is a way of practicing having a wide or narrow attention. Tuning into the body brings us into the present moment and diverts attention from thinking.

being with others

Practice being fully present with others.

• **Avoid checking your phone while in conversation.**

• **Notice whenever your mind wanders and bring it back to being here right now.**

• **Repeat!**

What do you notice?

It often happens that when we are with others, we are present in body but our mind is miles away. Notice what it feels like when you are with someone who is mentally far away.

Practice being fully present with family, friends, colleagues, and strangers. Experiment and notice how it affects your relationships.

letting things unfold

Notice when you have an expectation of a particular outcome. Notice how you feel if things turn out differently.

Whatever the outcome, be curious about what arises:

• in the head

• in the heart

• in the body.

What do you notice?

Expectations can box us into a single outcome. If there is a different result, we can feel disappointed, yet this might be unfounded. If we can allow things to unfold, we remain open to the myriad possibilities that might arise—ones that have not even occurred to us.

practicing self-compassion

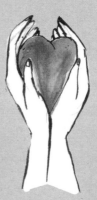

Whenever you are struggling:

Step 1: Acknowledge how you are feeling (head, heart, body).

Step 2: Acknowledge that others are suffering as you are—you are not alone in struggling.

Step 3: Silently repeat, "May I be kind to myself," or similar words.

Step 4: Make an intention to be compassionate toward yourself.

Let go of expecting to feel a particular way.

Realizing we are not alone in our suffering can make it less personal. Someone, somewhere, is going through what you are experiencing. It is the human condition.

25 PRACTICE

stop on red

Today, red means "Stop." Whenever you see the color red, such as a traffic light, a car, a toy, or on a tube of toothpaste, use it to remind you to pause.

Stop and tune into the breath.

Where do you feel the breath most strongly?

• **Belly?**

• **Chest?**

• **Upper lip?**

Stay with the sensations of breathing for a minute or so.

One of the hardest things about practicing mindfulness is remembering to do it. Tagging a practice to prompts, such as a particular color, can be helpful.

the gift of silence

Find some space for silence—**5 minutes, 10,** or longer.

Turn off the radio or TV and set aside your phone and any other devices.

Perhaps sit and watch the breath, or continue with what you are doing, but in silence and with awareness.

We often fill our days with "noise," but falling silent allows us to open up to whatever is here. Sometimes that may be connecting with our environment or inner world.

The lack of distraction shines a light on what is present—and that may not be pleasant. Remember to take care of yourself (see page 45).

REFLECT ON YOUR EXPERIENCE

Make a note here of the activities and practices you have tried, and how you have felt about them. You can write down why or if there is a particular time when they are helpful. You can then revisit this list for ideas on mindful activities and practices to try.

FIND OUT MORE

ORGANIZATIONS

Centre for Mindfulness Research & Practice (CMRP), Bangor, North Wales, UK
As well as professional training, the CMRP offers mindfulness teaching and retreats to the general public.
www.bangor.ac.uk/mindfulness

Oxford Mindfulness Centre, Oxford, UK
Offers professional training as well as mindfulness courses for the general public.
http://oxfordmindfulness.org

Be Mindful
The Mental Health Foundation's resource on mindfulness including UK teacher listings, information, and an online course.
http://bemindful.co.uk

Center for Mindfulness in Medicine, Health Care, and Society, Massachusetts, USA
Resources, professional training, and courses for the general public.
www.umassmed.edu/cfm

Sounds True
An excellent resource for purchasing audio CDs and downloads on mindfulness and other topics around personal transformation.
www.soundstrue.com

BOOKS

Buddha's Brain: The Practical Neuroscience of Happiness, Love and Wisdom by Rick Hanson and Daniel J. Siegel (New Harbinger Publications, 2009)

Full Catastrophe Living (Revised Edition) by Jon Kabat-Zinn (Piatkus, 2013)

The Mindful Path to Self Compassion: Freeing Yourself from Destructive Thoughts and Emotions by Christopher Germer (The Guilford Press, 2009)

The Mindful Way Through Depression by Mark Williams, John Teasdale, Zindel Segal, and Jon Kabat-Zinn (The Guilford Press, 2007)

Mindfulness: A Practical Guide to Finding Peace in a Frantic World by Professor Mark Williams and Dr Danny Penman (Piatkus, 2011)

Mindfulness for Health: A Practical Guide for Relieving Pain, Reducing Stress and Restoring Wellbeing by Vidyamala Burch and Dr Danny Penman (Piatkus, 2013)

Mindfulness in Eight Weeks: The Revolutionary 8-week Plan to Clear Your Mind and Calm Your Life by Michael Chaskalson (Harper Thorsons, 2014)

Self Compassion by Kristin Neff (Hodder & Stoughton, 2011)

Wherever You Go, There You Are: Mindfulness Meditation for Everyday Life by Jon Kabat-Zinn (Piatkus, 2004)

Other authors you may like to explore include Jack Kornfield, Sharon Salzberg, Joseph Goldstein, and Pema Chodron.

INDEX

acceptance 15
acknowledgment
   of the body 102
   of the head 103
   of the heart 104
amygdala 13, 17, 18
appreciating the good 70
approach mode 32, 33, 37
attention
   how we pay attention 10
   improving attention 16
   taking your attention to 27
attitudes, core 36–43
avoidance mode 32, 33, 37
awareness
   breath awareness 111
   light of awareness 23
   sensory awareness 16

banking the good 69
beginners
   beginner's mind 36, 41
   willingness to be a beginner 81
behavior, when stressed 92
Being With 29, 30–1
being with others 117
bigger picture, seeing the 16, 20
body
   acknowledging the body 102
   body scans 11, 116
   Breath and Body 56–7
   coming into the body 108
   outlining the body 109
   Power of the Body 32–3

tuning into body posture 110
breath and breathing 23
   breath awareness 111
   Breath and Body 56–7
   breathing into 26
   counting the breath 113
   just a minute 114
   letting go 115
   power of the breath 24–5
   stop on red 120
   taking a breathing space 112
   Watching the Breath 25, 50, 52–5
Buddhism 12
butterflies, stomach 18

caring for yourself 45, 76
children, mindfulness and 10
compassion, practicing self- 119
connection to the earth 107
cortisol 17, 18
creativity 20
crying 20
curiosity 37, 40, 41, 50, 84

depression 12, 32
detoxification, technology 94
different things, doing 83
digestive system, stomach
   butterflies and 18
discomfort, physical 50–1

early warning systems 15
earth, connecting to the 107

eating
   eating mindfully 11, 16
   eating something you don't like 101
emotions 32, 33
exercise 20
expectations
   letting go of 41
   letting things unfold 118
experiences
   how we perceive 14
   teasing apart your experience 22
   turning toward all experience 28–9
eyes 47

fight or flight response 17–18
five plus five 116
focus
   focusing on one thing 79
   improving focus 16
formal practice 44
future, back from the 86

good things
   appreciating the good 70
   banking the good 69
   good news 71

head, acknowledging the 103
healthy eating 20
heart, acknowledging the 104
hormones, stress 17, 18, 20

impulse of social media, noticing the 93
in service to others 87
informal practice 45
intention 47
  power of 66, 77
  setting 66, 78
itches, scratching 51, 57

judgment, non- 37, 38
just one thing, focusing on 79

Kabat-Zinn, Dr. Jon 12
kindness 37, 38–9
  random acts of 73
  self-kindness 16, 51

left prefrontal cortex 32, 33
letting go 14–15, 41, 115
light of awareness 23
looking after yourself 31
lying down 47

meditations 11, 20
  acknowledgment 102–4
  being with others 117
  body scan 116
  breath awareness 111
  Breath and Body 56–7
  coming into the body 108
  connecting to the earth 107
  counting the breath 113
  eating something you don't
    like 101

exploring the senses 96–100
five plus five 116
the gift of silence 121
just a minute 114
letting go 115
letting things unfold 118
Opening to Sounds 58–9
outlining the body 109
patience and 43
posture 46–7
practicing self-compassion 119
standing like a mountain 105
stop on red 120
taking a breathing space 112
tuning into the body posture
  110
walk, knowing that you are
  walking 106
Walking Practice 60–1
Watching the Breath 25, 52–5
mind, wandering 48–9, 54
mindfulness
  definition 10–11
  how mindfulness can help
    13–21
  origins of 12
  practicing 44–5
Mindfulness-Based Cognitive
  Therapy (MBCT) 12
Mindfulness-Based Stress
  Reduction (MBSR) 12
mountain, standing like 105

narrative, noticing the 34–5
nature 20
negative thinking 34, 48
news, good 71
non-judgment 37, 38
non-striving 42
nourishment 39

Opening to Sounds 58–9

patience 43
perspective 16, 20
  taking a different perspective 85
physical discomfort 50–1
posture, tuning into body 110
Power of the Body 32–3
practices, core 52–61
pushing buttons, what pushes
  your buttons 89

random acts of kindness 73
right prefrontal cortex 32

scratching the itch 51, 57
self-care 45, 75
self-compassion, practicing 119
self-help 19–20
senses, exploring 96–100
sensory awareness 16
sight, exploring 96
silence, gift of 121
sitting 46
smell, exploring 97
smiling inside 72

social media 93

sounds, exploring 98

space, creating 80

standing 47

   standing like a mountain 105

stop on red 120

stress 17–21

   chronic stress 18–19

   how you behave when
     stressed 92

   reducing stress 13

   self-help 19–20

   stress reaction 17–18

   what does stress feel like 90

   what helps when you are
     stressed 91

suffering, letting go of 14–15

talking 20

taste, exploring 99

technology detox 94

tension 14–15, 32

thoughts

   negative thinking 34, 48

   thought process 34–5

   "thought tone" 38

time, making the most of 67

touch, exploring 100

tourists, being 82

treatment

   how you treat others 74

   how you treat yourself 75

tuning into 27

   tuning in to the body 32–3, 34

unpleasant things, noticing 88

waking up to life 15

walking, knowing that you are
   walking 106

Walking Practice 23, 60–1

wandering mind 48–9, 54

Watching the Breath 25, 50, 52–5

Williams, Mark 35

willingness to be a beginner 81

ACKNOWLEDGMENTS

Many thanks to Cindy Richards, Carmel Edmonds, and the team at
CICO Books for all their hard work and support, to Helen Ridge for
her editing, to Emily Breen for the design, and to Amy Louise Evans for
her terrific illustrations.

Many thanks also to Eluned Gold, Melissa Blacker, and David Rynick for
your ongoing support and encouragement. Thank you to my family and
friends (you know who you are) for always being there for me. Particular
thanks to those who have shown up to my classes, have committed to the
practice, and continue to be such amazing teachers for me. Thank you.